Luis Oerter

The Environmental Work of Al Gore

GRIN Verlag

Bibliografische Information der Deutschen Nationalbibliothek:

Die Deutsche Bibliothek verzeichnet diese Publikation in der Deutschen National-
bibliografie; detaillierte bibliografische Daten sind im Internet über http://dnb.d-
nb.de/ abrufbar.

Impressum:

Copyright © 2012 GRIN Verlag GmbH
Druck und Bindung: Books on Demand GmbH, Norderstedt Germany
ISBN: 978-3-656-47070-0

Dieses Buch bei GRIN:

http://www.grin.com/de/e-book/230673/the-environmental-work-of-al-gore

GRIN - Your knowledge has value

Der GRIN Verlag publiziert seit 1998 wissenschaftliche Arbeiten von Studenten, Hochschullehrern und anderen Akademikern als eBook und gedrucktes Buch. Die Verlagswebsite www.grin.com ist die ideale Plattform zur Veröffentlichung von Hausarbeiten, Abschlussarbeiten, wissenschaftlichen Aufsätzen, Dissertationen und Fachbüchern.

Besuchen Sie uns im Internet:

http://www.grin.com/

http://www.facebook.com/grincom

http://www.twitter.com/grin_com

Reichsstadt-Gymnasium
Rothenburg ob der Tauber

Abiturjahrgang
2010/12

Seminararbeit

zum wissenschaftspropädeutischen Seminar mit dem Rahmenthema

'America Going Green'

im Leitfach Englisch

Thema der Arbeit

The Environmental Work of Al Gore

Copyright Luis Oerter

Verfasser: Luis Oerter

1. Introduction

The United States of America have always had a tremendous influence on other countries and were often a few steps ahead in many important scientific developments. However, it took a long time for Americans to realize the issue of climate change but now America has finally started "going green". But what does "going green" mean? First of all it is about reducing the consumption of energy all over the world in order to lower CO_2-emissions. Carbon dioxide is one of the greenhouse gases that cause more energy of the sunlight to stay in the Earth's atmosphere than normal. Due to this process we have higher temperatures and more extreme weather situations. Possible solutions for the climate crisis can be fuel efficient- or electric cars and renewable energies like solar- or wind energy. Although many steps have already been taken, the world still has a long way to go if climate change is supposed to be decelerated. With a quarter of all CO_2-emissions worldwide the USA have an important function in the fight against global warming, which can be in danger without their help.

The man who made many Americans change their mind about environmental protection and a "green" lifestyle is Al Gore. But how did one man change almost a whole nation's thinking about an uncomfortable topic they had ignored so far? Even as Senator of Tennessee and Vice President of the USA, Gore had to fight hard for his environmental goals. His commitment to trying to change the world and his love for nature are impressive. These traits enable him to give passionate speeches having the power to make people want to save our environment. Unlike many other politicians, he continued his attempts to change the world after his time in office and was far more successful. Considering the great impression Gore made on people all over the world, the following question comes up: " What did Al Gore do – and still does - to save our environment?" To answer this question one has to have a closer look at the man himself investigating his personal background and political career.

2. Al Gore's Childhood and Education

2.1 Early Years and School

Albert Arnold "Al" Gore Junior was born on 31st March 1948 in Washington D.C. Because of his father's political career, he spent his childhood partly in Washington D.C. and in Carthage, Tennessee, where his father was Senator. It is said that Al Gore's political career began the day after his birth. He was on the first page of the local newspaper "Tennessean". His father had asked the publisher to put him there in order to enhance his own popularity. From then on most of the decisions in Gore´s life were made on behalf of his political career. Although he moved to Washington D.C. when he started secondary school, he still had to work at the family farm so he would be a credible "boy from the South". Gore probably made his first "green" experiences working there. [1] Later he went to St. Albans, an expensive and exclusive preperatory school, where most of the powerful families sent their children. His schoolmates had famous names like Bush, Kennedy or Roosevelt[2] and were sent there for the same reason as Gore: learning how to be a politician.[3]

2.2 Harvard and Military Service

After graduating from St. Albans he applied to Harvard in 1965 and was immediately admitted because of his father´s connections despite the fact that his grades were only average. The subject he chose was political sciences.[4] Although he was strictly opposed to the Vietnam War, Gore joined the United States Army soon after receiving his university degree in 1969. But Gore was not found at the front. He used his time in Vietnam to work as a journalist and never participated in any battles.[5] When Gore had returned from Vietnam in 1971, he had his first crisis working up the new experiences. He decided to go to college again and this time he chose theology

---

[1] cf. Stefan Kornelius, *Al Gore - Mission Klima*, Freiburg im Breisgau, Herder, 2000, p.17.
[2] Families of three former US-Presidents.
[3] cf. Ibid., pp. 21-22.
[4] cf. Ibid., p. 24.
[5] cf. Peter Neumann, *Al Gore – Eine Biographie*, Stuttgart, Deutsche Verlags-Anstalt   GmbH, 2000, p. 44, p. 47.

as a subject. "These studies helped me asking the right questions.", as he stated in hindsight. It is also important to highlight that: "more importantly they gave him an understanding of environmental politics."[6]

3. Al Gore Starting a Political Career and Environmental Activism

3.1 The House of Representatives and Senatorial Dignity

In 1976 Al Gore decided to run for a seat in the United States House of Representatives, the lower legislative house of the United States Congress and succeeded. In the first two years he was able to win a few smaller arguments, which meant good publicity and solidified his position in Congress[7]. At that time he was not representing his thoughts referring to environmentalism yet, because hardly anyone cared for this or similar topics. The first time he had to deal with pollution of the environment was in 1978, when a company disposed poisonous industrial waste near a residential district. But although he brought draft proposals to Congress, which should forbid such disposal sites, his behaviour in Congress was not very straight. Gore could not allow himself to provoke the industry, so he slightly went back on his proposals. When he was Senator of Tennessee from 1985 to 1993, Gore interrupted his environmental work.[8]

3.2 First Run for Presidency

As soon as Al Gore had decided to run for 1988´s presidency his "green" goals were excluded from his election programme. This was, as he admitted later, the biggest mistake of modern Democrats: Selling out sustainability for short range political targets. Gore's untrustworthy behaviour caused many environmentalist voters to be very disappointed in him. That disappointment surely affected the voters' decisions and

---

[6] Quoted as in Peter Neumann, *Al Gore – Eine Biographie*, Stuttgart, Deutsche Verlags-Anstalt GmbH, 2000, p.52.

[7] cf. Peter Neumann, *Al Gore – Eine Biographie, Stuttgart*, Deutsche Verlags-Anstalt GmbH, 2000, pp. 58-59.

[8] cf. Peter Neumann, *Al Gore – Eine Biographie*, Stuttgart, Deutsche Verlags-Anstalt GmbH, 2000, pp.70-71.

perhaps he would not have lost the Democrats' primary if he had stayed true to his political principles.[9]

3.3 Earth in Balance

In 1989 Al Gore had to face a severe stroke of fate. After family and friends of his had visited a baseball game, his son Albert III was hit by a car and was only able to survive by the immediate help of two nurses. The accident in combination with the week-long fear for Albert's life somehow brought Gore closer to environmental protection again.[10] In order to master his personal crisis, he tried to help the Earth fight its. "Earth in Balance – Ecology and the Human Spirit"[11] was the name of the book he started to write soon after his son's accident. "The leading theme of the book is the global environmental crisis, which according to Gore questions the continued existence of our civilisation in its present form".[12] The book is subdivided into three parts. In the first part Gore points out how seriously the Earth and especially living creatures will be affected by global warming and other climate changes. He also adds that the climate changes caused by humans are by far more extreme than natural changes. The second part explains how mankind was able to ignore the prognostic symptoms of an environmental catastrophe. Gore blames the economy for hiding the ecologically harmful aspects of its actions. Another reason for ignoring the danger can be found in the human race's overestimation of its own power, that leads to gluttony. Finally, Gore detects that the origin of the urge to control and exploit nature can be found in ancient Greece and was continued by Judaism and Christianity until today. A way to delay global warming is presented in the third and last part of "Earth in Balance". The fight against climate changes shall become "the main organisational principle of our civilisation", like the fight against Communism until the end of the Cold War. Gore's plan includes five targets: firstly stabilizing the population number in the Third World by raising the level of literacy and informing about birth control,

---

[9] cf. Peter Neumann, *Al Gore – Eine Biographie*, Stuttgart, Deutsche Verlags-Anstalt GmbH, 2000, pp. 84-87.
[10] cf. Stefan Kornelius, *Al Gore - Mission Klima*, Freiburg im Breisgau, Herder, 2000, pp.57-58.
[11] Published in 1992.
[12] cf. Peter Neumann, *Al Gore – Eine Biographie*, Stuttgart, Deutsche Verlags-Anstalt GmbH, 2000, p.88.

secondly developing environmentally friendly technologies (especially an alternative to the combustion-engine) and thirdly charging fees for environmental pollution. The fourth goal was to form treaties with other countries in order to protect the environment and last but not least international communication of pollution-data was planned as the fifth goal. Altogether the book was supposed to present a global Marshallplan[13] that was able to save the Earth. When the book was published, people were amazed by the way he made the topic popular in public[4]. After a short time Gore and his ideas were even more famous than before.

4. Gore as Vice President

4.1 The Rio Summit

While Gore focused on working on his book "Earth in Balance", his political career stagnated, although he still was Senator of Tennessee. Visiting the Arctic, the rainforest and other endangered territories was more important to him and a second presidential run was out of the question. At the climate summit in Rio de Janeiro in 1992 Gore tried to convince the leader of the American delegation to sign treaties for environmental protection, but neither the treaty protecting endangered species, nor the "United Nations Framework Convention on Climate Change - the first international agreement to declare the climate change a serious problem and to bind the United Nations to take action."[15] - were signed by the USA.[16]

4.2 "Green Gore" in the White House

Although Al Gore did not become President in 1992, he was able to get an office in the White House. Bill Clinton made him a last-minute offer to become Vice President

---

[13] "Economic recovery plan designed and implemented by the United States to assist with recovery efforts for Western Europe after World War II." http://www.investorworcs.com

[14] cf. Peter Neumann, *Al Gore – Eine Biographie*, Stuttgart, Deutsche Verlags-Anstalt GmbH, 2000, pp.89-92.

[15] http://www.bmu.de/klimaschutz/internationale_klimapolitik/glossar/doc/2902.php#klimarahmen p .5.

[16] cf. Peter Neumann, *Al Gore – Eine Biographie*, Stuttgart, Deutsche Verlags-Anstalt GmbH, 2000,pp. 97-98.

and expectedly Gore grabbed the chance to take another step on the career ladder. Clinton generously made him responsible for many important departments and one of them was environmental protection. As many environmentalists had hoped, Gore asserted major personnel changes in this section and some of them were even made government workers. [17] Clinton refused to raise taxes on oil and coal, but initiated lower taxes on the less polluting gas. As soon as Gore had managed to free renewable energies from taxes, many environmentalists were very satisfied with this new Vice President. But the next setback was not long in coming. Shortly after the new tax laws were introduced, the Republicans protested fiercely against the tax raises and so the law was turned down again. This was especially harmful to Gore's environmentalism, because keeping the pollution at bay by charging fees was a very decisive point in his plan to save the Earth. Experiencing this defeat may have disillusioned Al Gore politically, since he went without public initiatives afterwards. In 1993 Bill Clinton signed the United Nations Framework Convention on Climate Change, which was only "a symbolic act without consequences". In the following years of Clinton's presidency, Gore always made decisions with respect to protecting the environment, but the CO_2-emissions did not stop increasing. The government's 50-point-plan was in a certain way superficial, filled with tips for the Americans to reduce their emission of greenhouse gases.[18]

4.3   Second Legislative Period as Vice President

4.3.1 Gentle Environmentalism

During the next election campaign for 1996, Al Gore reinforced his green goals by making the improvement of quality of living coming along with many little measures protecting the environment clear to people. Clinton and Gore were still "[...] talking about a global Marshallplan, but the keen rhethoric clearly contradicted the actual actions.[...] Many environmentalists complained that Clinton and Gore, who had

---

[17] cf. Peter Neumann, *Al Gore – Eine Biographie*, Stuttgart, Deutsche Verlags-Anstalt GmbH, 2000,p.111.

[18] Peter Neumann, *Al Gore – Eine Biographie*, Stuttgart, Deutsche Verlags-Anstalt GmbH,   2000, pp. 112-113.

stepped up as an 'environmental government' [...]" did no longer deserve that name and were just as little green as their predecessors. Despite these accusations, "[...] the Vice President worked on the enforcement of his eco-political agenda continuously, even if it happened by slow degrees and without the attention of the public at large." He was able to add environmental protection to the definition of national security and he achieved to tighten the laws for air pollution, although the industry was – as it had to be expected – very displeased about it. The people were supposed to receive tax exemptions for using "low-emission-cars" and producing renewable energy.[19] Therefore, Gore was probably the best Vice President environmentalists could have had at that point of time.

4.3.2 The Kyoto Summit

"The most important event of [Gore's] second term of office was doubtlessly the climate summit in Kyoto, Japan" which was held in 1997. The main topic of the summit was also a major aim of Gore's Marshallplan: "arranging international rules in order to reduce greenhouse gas-emissions and thereby damming back global warming".[20] Despite many industrial anti-environmentalists and several delegations of countries with emerging economies he was able to convince 38 industrial nations to sign an agreement which obliged them to reduce or retain their emission rates in comparison to 1990. If a nation polluted the air even less than it had announced before, it was allowed to sell the left over emission-rights to another nation struggling to reach its own target. [21]

But the majority of Americans once again denied to accept higher gas prices, a possibly weaker economy and huge investments in eco-friendly technologies. In August

---

[19] cf. Peter Neumann, *Al Gore – Eine Biographie*, Stuttgart, Deutsche Verlags-Anstalt GmbH,   2000, pp. 143-145.
[20] cf. Peter Neumann, *Al Gore – Eine Biographie*, Stuttgart, Deutsche Verlags-Anstalt GmbH,   2000, p.145.
[21] cf. Peter Neumann, *Al Gore – Eine Biographie*, Stuttgart, Deutsche Verlags-Anstalt GmbH,   2000, pp. 146-152.

1998 the treaty was declared inconvertible and was shifted to the year 2001. Thus, Clinton did not have to care about it any more. [22]

5.   Al Gore's Life after Vice Presidency

5.1 Second Presidential Run

The decision to run for presidency in 2000 was definitely not a political surprise after two terms in office as Vice President. Environmental protection was still very important to him, but

> Gore's campaign consultants had advised him to avoid talking about the environment because it wasn't a first-tier issue. What they missed was that it moved Gore and allowed him to demonstrate his leadership. By depriving him of his most effective passion, they weakened him as a candidate. Gore lost the 2000 election in part because he came across as a robotic candidate. After the election, [he] began speaking out on the environment with a passion that electrified audiences.[23]

This was especially shown, when he started working on a campaign showing his slide show about climate change after the lost election. While he could hardly move anyone emotionally during the election campaign[24], training younger co-workers how to convey the necessity of environmental protection was easy for him.[25]

5.2   Environmental Projects

5.2.1 Generation Investment Management

Generation Investment Management (GIM) is an investment company Gore founded together with David Blood in 2004.[26] The company is supposed to protect the environment firstly by using eco-friendly technologies in its offices and secondly - and also more importantly - by investing in a way that provides sustainability. Technologies like hybrid-cars, biofuels and efficient building design are in the field of in-

[22] cf. Peter Neumann, *Al Gore – Eine Biographie*, Stuttgart, Deutsche Verlags-Anstalt GmbH,   2000, p. 154.
[23] Quoted as in http://www.ontheissues.org/Archive/Obama_Challenge_Al_Gore.htm, p.1.
[24] cf. Stefan Kornelius, *Al Gore - Mission Klima*, Freiburg im Breisgau, Herder, 2000, p. 80.
[25] cf. Stefan Kornelius, *Al Gore - Mission Klima*, Freiburg im Breisgau, Herder, 2000, pp. 118- 119
[26] cf. Peter Neumann, *Al Gore – Eine Biographie*, Stuttgart, Deutsche Verlags-Anstalt GmbH, 2000, pp.98-99.

terests of GIM.[27] The minimum investment period is three years, which shows that long-term-investment is intended.[28]

5.3 An Inconvenient Truth

The story of Gore's Oscar-winning documentary film starts in 1989, when he presented his position on climate change as Senator in Washington using a slide show. In 2001 his wife Tipper encouraged him to digitalize it and so a multimedia presentation was created.[29] The presentation was later made into a film because of its success and emotionality. Instead of talking about environmental problems in a technical an complex way, Gore uses a kind of language everybody can understand. Gore focuses moreover on one major problem everyone can be affected by: global warming. The personal stories taken from his own life touch people's heart and together with the impressive pictures they suddenly make global warming seizable. Shooting the film was simple. A studio with a stage and a giant screen, where Gore gave his lecture three times, was set up. After that the material was "[...] cut and edited dramaturgically".[30]

Although Gore's film was a huge success, it can not be denied that it also had certain weaknesses.

> For a climate-politically interested person, the content of the film is rather disappointing [...]: rising temperatures due to the greenhouse effect, a higher number of extreme weather situations, the glacial recession and the Arctic melt, the resulting rise of the sea level and the decreasing ocean salinity with possible consequences for the big ocean currents. Gore connects the climatic phenomena to a single apocalyptic scenario and conveys the feeling, that doom is imminent.[31]

In case the film was shown in class, the government insisted on pointing out nine mistakes in the film. Especially the fact that Gore shows the rise of the sea level as if

---

[27] cf. www.generationim.com

[28] cf. Peter Neumann, *Al Gore – Eine Biographie*, Stuttgart, Deutsche Verlags-Anstalt GmbH, 2000, pp.98-99.

[29] cf. Peter Neumann, *Al Gore – Eine Biographie*, Stuttgart, Deutsche Verlags-Anstalt GmbH, 2000, pp.98-100.

[30] cf. Stefan Kornelius, *Al Gore - Mission Klima*, Freiburg im Breisgau, Herder, 2000, p. 120.

[31] Stefan Kornelius, *Al Gore - Mission Klima*, Freiburg im Breisgau, Herder, 2000, p. 120.

it could happen in a few days is wrong. The procedure would take at least a hundred years. It is also not proven that the hurricane Katrina[32] was intensified by global warming, as he claims in his presentation. [33]Nevertheless, the film was a huge success and reached millions of people. Gore had finally managed to spread his message all over the USA. He even published three books relating to the film: one simply showing the presentation on paper, another one for young adults and a third one for children.

"The film brought in 24 million dollars and became the third most successful documentary film in history – after "Fahrenheit 9/11" [...] and "March of the Penguins"[...]."[34] Although Gore could actually not receive the Oscar as main actor of the film[35], he was the one shown on the red carpet and on stage. Despite his new popularity and many people hoping that he would run for Presidency in 2008 Al Gore decided not to try it.[36]

5.4   Live Earth

Live Earth was a project initiated by Al Gore. Twelve benefit concerts were planned to be given on all seven continents on the same day in 2007 and the profit was supposed to be used for environmental protection. But the success of the event was very questionable because of several reasons. Some of the concerts did not have enough spectators and the concert in Rio de Janeiro was said to be ecologically harmful. Altogether the project was not the big success Gore had hoped for. His critics measured him by his own standards and also complained about the amount of energy he used with his private jet and his limousines.[37]

---

[32] A hurricane, which destroyed and flooded New Orleans badly 2005.
[33] cf. Stefan Kornelius, *Al Gore - Mission Klima*, Freiburg im Breisgau, Herder, 2000, p. 121.
[34] cf. Stefan Kornelius, *Al Gore - Mission Klima*, Freiburg im Breisgau, Herder, 2000, p. 122.
[35] The Oscar for the best documentary film is usually given to the director.
[36] cf. Stefan Kornelius, *Al Gore - Mission Klima*, Freiburg im Breisgau, Herder, 2000, pp. 135-   137.
[37] cf. Stefan Kornelius, *Al Gore - Mission Klima*, Freiburg im Breisgau, Herder, 2000, pp. 140-   142

6. Conclusion

Despite his critics Al Gore has really made a difference in the fight against climate change and his alleged hypocrisy is very questionable. Every time he has to travel by aircraft he buys a carbon offset to make up for it.[38] Considering the effort Gore has made in order to help people understand the importance of environmental protection one could say that he justifiably received the Nobel Peace Prize in 2007 together with the Intergovernmental Panel on Climate Change for "their efforts to build up and disseminate greater knowledge about man-made climate change, and to lay the foundations for the measures that are needed to counteract such change". Unlike the Nobel Prizes in physics, medicine, literature etc. the Nobel Peace Prize also delivers a political message. By choosing Al Gore as prize winner the committee ranged him on a level as for example Martin Luther King, Mother Teresa or Nelson Mandela. Gore donated his share of the prize money to the Alliance for Climate Protection – an organisation he had founded in 2006.

Being a wealthy man, Gore invests in making his lifestyle "greener". All his family members drive hybrid-cars and his mansion in Nashville, Tennessee has been rebuilt in order to make it as energy efficient as possible. The fact that he is already 63 years old and mankind is nowhere near realizing the danger of climate change may make one wonder, who is supposed to continue Al Gore's environmental work. Although Gore has four children – who often follow in their parents' political footsteps in the USA - he will probably not have a successor among them. While two of his daughters have decided to become authoresses, Gore's son has made also negative headlines. In 2007 he was stopped because of speeding and caught with marijuana. Al Gore's environmental heritage is more likely to be apportioned among several younger environmentalists. Additionally, there are several institutions whose targets are the same as Gore's, with some of them even having been founded by him. Even though Al Gore has not saved the world yet, he succeeded in changing Americans' – and other people's – attitude towards environmental protection significantly. Furthermore it is worth mentioning that Gore made environmentalism a relevant or even central

---

[38] Carbon offsets are certificates for investing in projects which help to reduce greenhouse gas-emissions. This system works, because to the global climate it does not matter where on Earth the pollution occurs.

political issue in the USA. Even some Republicans, as for example Arnold Schwar-
zenegger now deal with "green" ideas. This can also be regarded as Al Gore's contri-
bution to the process of "America going green".

7. Bibliography

7.1 Books

Kornelius, Stefan, *Al Gore – Mission Klima*, Freiburg im Breisgau, Herder, 2000

Neumann, Peter, *Al Gore – Eine Biographie*, Stuttgart, Deutsche Verlags-Anstalt
GmbH, 2000

7.2 Weblinks

BMU – Klimaschutz : Glossar,
http://www.bmu.de/klimaschutz/internationale_klimapolitik/glossar/doc/2902.php#kl
imarahmen, p. 5, 14.10.2011

Climate Change Investment Implications of a Systems View, http://www.generationim.-
com/sustainability/challenges/climate-change.html, p.1, 03.11.2011

Environment, http://www.generationim.com/citizenship/environment.html, 03.11.2011

Kuttner, Robert,
http://www.ontheissues.org/Archive/Obama_Challenge_Al_Gore.htm, p.1,
21.10.2011

What is Marshall Plan? definition and meaning,
http://www.investorwords.com/7673/Marshall_Plan.html, 19.10.2011